# FANTASTICAL : TALES OF

## BEARS, BEER AND HEMOPHILIA

D1301435

# FANTASTICAL

# TALES OF
## BEARS, BEER AND
## HEMOPHILIA

Marija Bulatovic

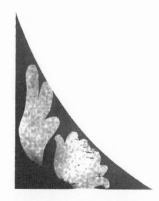

SOL, LLC.

Published by SOL, LLC.
Printed in the United States of America
First Edition

Paperback ISBN: 978-0-9904106-1-4
eBook ISBN: 978-0-9904106-3-8
Cover and interior art design by Nina Bojovic
Interior layout by Anne LoCascio

*To my grandparents, who loved me so perfectly and so well.*

*To my parents, my faithful guides and eternal strength.*

*To my son, my inspiration and my heart.*

*To my husband, my love.*

# Acknowledgments

This book, like much of life, would not have been possible without a little magic—the magic of the stories themselves, the magic of memory, and the magic of the incredible people around me who helped bring it all to life.

First and foremost, I thank my family. I can always count on my loving and amazing parents for their unwavering support, loyalty, and enthusiasm. This case has been no different. My parents encouraged me from the start and were kind enough to allow me to share these stories—stories of their past, their families, and their lives—with a wider audience.

I also owe my deepest thanks to my husband. He cheered me on with each new tale, delighting in hearing every single one. He also helped me see the big picture, tirelessly playing out various ways of ordering the stories and positioning the manuscript. He has been my trusted advisor on this journey, always encouraging me to keep investing in the project and always the first to laugh out loud at the fourth, fifth, even eighth, iteration of a story.

My son was the inspiration and catalyst for this book. His birth, and the maze of parenthood that followed, drew me to my past and led me to reflect on how my parents, their parents, and others before me had carried out this most glorious and momentous role. It was through this journey back, this quest for the wisdom and experience of my elders, that I stumbled upon my own childhood and these stories.

Finally, I thank my grandparents, who lived the majority of this book alongside me, and who, from my earliest days, shared so generously of themselves, their lives, and their rich histories.

Beyond my family, I thank my first reader, our wonderful *au pair* Courtney Schnettler. Courtney read the stories with great interest, embraced them, and always provided a fresh perspective when I needed one. I'll never forget the two of us sitting around the kitchen table, me pumping breast milk and regaling her with the story of my past and her listening attentively, sharing her easy, kind laughter in return.

My sincerest thanks also go to my dear friend and adviser, Joe Keller. Joe traveled the self-publishing path before me and has proven, time and again, an excellent guide. Joe always found time to address my questions and help me navigate, and he always put good energy out into the universe for me and this project. I could never have come this far without him.

It was my cover illustrator, Nina Bojovic, who gave the book a face—bringing to life a dancing bear, a young narrator, gypsies, and the magic of Yugoslavia in the '80s. I thank Nina for her incredible creativity, patience, and professionalism. She was a true joy to work with, and I continue to be amazed at her skill in envisioning and molding my concepts and stories into life.

Finally, I thank the broader circle of family, friends, and professionals who have contributed to and continue to sustain this project. Their support has been incredibly valuable.

It is through the magic of these incredible people—their love, kindness, skills, and talent—that these stories have come to be written and shared. My sincere thanks to all who have touched this project!

*My parents on their wedding day, Yugoslavia, 1975*

# Contents

# INTRODUCTION

*The gypsy woman shuffled the cards, blew on them, and cast them down, carefully, deliberately, with the skilled hand of a weaver of life and magic:*

*You will travel the world,*
*A child will make you proud,*
*You will marry a businessman, but you will still work to make your own way,*
*You will live a life of adventure…*

*—Kraljevo, 1993*

The Yugoslavia of my childhood was anything but dull. A fantastical place rich in history, populated with intense people, and shot through with wonders and deep emotions, it was part of the Balkans, otherwise known as the powder keg of Europe. It was the birthplace of diverse luminaries—from Nikola Tesla, inventor of modern alternating current, to Anjezë Gonxhe Bojaxhiu, the Albanian nun who would become Mother Teresa, to top tennis star Novak Djokovic.

Touching Austria to the North, Italy and the Adriatic to the West, Greece to the South, and Romania and Bulgaria to the East, it was the place that started World War I, that pioneered its own grand experiment in socialism, and that would later be home to the infamous ethnic cleansing of the '90s and some of the most sought-after mass murderers on the planet.

Given its strategic location, it had been in the path of many conquerors. Everyone from the Visigoths to the Ottomans to the Austro-Hungarians to Soviet-era Communists had traversed its beautiful lands, leaving parts of their customs, language, and DNA behind.

The Ottomans brought foods and spices, the rhythms of the East, Islam. The Austro-Hungarians imparted Western European tastes, their own musical preferences, and industrial-age improvements. Finally, the Communists, the great equalizers of the diverse groups of people who now called this land home, were probably most responsible for the feeling of solidarity that I most strongly associate with it.

To me it was an amusing and intriguing place. Strange happenings, outrageous gossip, black magic—all were part of the fabric of my childhood, along with the safety and stability of home that was always there in the background, the love embodied in my parents, grandparents, and the larger circles of family and friends.

As I read back through these stories, the word "fantastical" sticks in my mind. Its meaning ranges from "existing in fancy only" to "slightly odd or even a bit weird." My Yugoslavian childhood was definitely both. These stories represent a lost world. Not only does the Yugoslav nation no longer exist, but the sense of solidarity among its peoples, giving way in the '80s and '90s to ethnic divisions and nationalist tendencies, will never be the same.

These stories also represent an odd world. In a young socialist country with pagan roots, ancient and modern worlds slammed together. The incongruities were sometimes jarring, sometimes hilarious. As a child, I tried continually to make sense of it all. As an adult, I feel lucky to have taken it all in. I feel fortunate to have had such a start in life—a strange start, perhaps, but one lived openly and in full color.

I sometimes describe my childhood as "socialist meets gypsy Woody Allen." When I was eleven, a nurse on her way to work one morning was stabbed in the back by a coworker. The two women worked together at the only hospital in our town and were part of a love triangle. In the end, no charges were filed, and the three lovers went back to work as usual. As local gossip had it, it was fortunate the event had taken place near the steps of the blood bank, ensuring rapid transfusion.

Others died each year in horrific bus crashes, caused by the regular drinking of drivers ferrying people to their chosen vacation destinations—or, in this case, to their deaths. Still others met their demise after eating poisonous mushrooms purchased at the local market. Apparently, the sellers couldn't tell the difference or just didn't care.

Especially in more remote parts of the country, a few people each year would barely escape being buried alive. Since no doctor was involved in validating death, the family would make the judgment on their own, sometimes mistakenly. The deceased would then be left to their own devices, forced to bang on the coffin lid in the midst of the funeral procession to be let out.

Needless to say, all this unpredictability fueled the superstitions harbored by many. At the same time, after more than thirty years of Communism, some things in Yugoslavia were *very* predictable. In our traditional, homogenous society, before the economic crisis that was to come, no one was too rich or too poor, no one too well or shabbily dressed. You could always count on some things to run smoothly and others not at all. A case in point was the *Yugo*. Voted one of the Fifty Worst Cars of All Time, it supposedly featured rear-window defrost so your hands wouldn't get cold while you pushed it.

The Yugoslavia of my memory was wonderfully diverse, and in my world, at least, its various ethnic and religious groups lived together in relative harmony.

Those around me were generally happy and satisfied with life, frequently socializing with friends and coworkers. The sense of solidarity was high. People wanted to do good and contribute to the overall benefit of society, and they generally looked out for one another.

I also remember a strong sense of intimacy, with people deeply involved in each other's lives. It was common for everyone to know what you were cooking for lunch, and should the aroma leave some question as to the exact dish, it was perfectly acceptable to ask and have your suspicions validated.

Growing up, it was my grandparents' world I was most familiar with and that colored my childhood. While my parents worked, I spent most days with my grandparents in the large apartment complex they shared with other military families in the Serbian city of Kraljevo. Communist-era buildings are typically presented as drab and gray, but I remember the balconies always beautifully adorned with plants and flowers, the interior walls always freshly painted in pastel colors. I also recall the complex teeming with people coming and going, providing abundant material for the local gossip.

Other stories reflect my parents' world, in Kraljevo and on the banks of the Adriatic where we vacationed each summer, still surrounded by family and friends. Their world, too, was caught up in tradition, elaborate social norms, and the remnants of a more superstitious time, but it gestured toward modernity.

Some of these stories come to me solely though

*Postcard from Kraljevo, 1955-1980*

the gossip of neighbors, embellished in their own minds and later, in mine. Some come through the lens of childhood, colored by my need to make sense of my own actions and an often confusing world. Still, this place and time—the Yugoslavia of my childhood—is real. Welcome, reader, to these tales of a time and place long gone, a world vanished from the map but not the mind. Join me on this journey and let your own reality dissolve.

# HANGING
## at the Day Care

My grandparents' apartment overlooked the main street of our town and the courtyard of the complex in which it was situated. As such, it provided an excellent view of the comings and goings of the townspeople and an opportunity for even closer scrutiny of the neighbors. Over the years, my grandparents had come to know everyone in the building, and everyone knew them. Neighbors had become acquaintances, and acquaintances had become friends for life.

People participated in each other's daily business, consulting one another on key decisions—whether to drive a *Lada* or a *Skoda*, which bank to keep their money in, which professors would show the most fairness in teaching their children. They discussed the most suitable romantic matches for themselves and others. They bathed dead neighbors in their own bathtubs and prepared them for their final voyage, then sat and comforted the families in their grief.

In this nearly idyllic setting, with everyone so deeply involved in each other's lives, it came as a shock one day when one of the complex's residents tried to kill himself. By all accounts, he was a quiet, stable man. He had two grown daughters and a grandson he and his wife cared for. My grandfather had served with him in the military, and his balcony faced ours. When the news broke one afternoon, everyone was shocked to their core—how could such a composed, seemingly happy man try to take his own life?

Some said it was his "type" that always cracked first. This explanation troubled me. Did my grandparents fit the bill? Should I expect the same from them? I resolved to follow the neighborhood gossip closely to learn more.

That evening we heard the full story. Earlier in the day, the man had tried to hang himself from a tree by the river. The neighbors played out the scene in their minds, speculating on the details of what must have been the man's larger plan— that the tree branch would eventually snap from the weight of his dead body and drop off into the turbulent waters of the river, that his corpse would be carried out of town, downstream and to the north. There, his body would decompose, but this was perhaps unlikely as the river's water was cold. Instead, he would be found floating in the next town, his lungs filled with air, or water, or both.

For myself, all I could think was—what a way to die, alone in the brisk winter wind. What a way to end, swinging from a tree branch in a desolate grove of the riverbank, awaiting even colder waters to wash you away.

As luck would have it, the man's plan was destined to fail. Apparently in our town, you can't even die alone. A local fisherman had seen him checking out the trees, looking for a sturdy one, and watched him as he prepared the noose and slipped it around his neck before leaping to his death.

But the man had selected a willow, with its long and flexible branches, and the tree was unable to support his weight. By the time the fisherman understood what was happening and rushed over to help, our neighbor was on the noose, dangling in the bitter cold water—half dead, half enraged, half screaming for help, half tightening the noose to finish himself off.

The man was eventually escorted home through the streets of our town in open daylight, his clothes soaking wet, one shoe gone, the noose still around his neck. The end of it was clutched in his hand as if in protest of life and of failure and perhaps an indication of his commitment to finish the job in the future.

But no one paid any attention. No one bothered to ask him why he had wanted to kill himself, thought about what had driven him to it, or even wondered how he could be helped. People just shook their heads, more and more of them saying that his type was simply prone to suicide. They moved on to the next piece of gossip, putting the shame he had brought to the neighborhood behind them.

For myself, I continued to ponder the meaning of it all. I checked on my grandparents regularly, making sure nothing that resembled a noose was being readied by the door and that no trips to the river were being planned.

The winter came to an end, and the first signs of spring were all around. The birds started to chirp again. The first flowers pushed their heads through the slim remnants of snow. The days grew longer, and people seemed happier. I, too, was uplifted by the generally optimistic, happy-go-lucky mood and the fresh life energy all around me. With no signs of strange behavior in my grandparents and other town gossip to distract me, I had nearly forgotten about the suicidal type and our neighbor's sad existence.

Then one Friday morning I heard the opening and shutting of doors in the building—people rushing from one apartment to the next, spreading some piece of news very quickly. They were shaking their heads, suppressing laughter, and following it with very serious looks.

Friday was one of two major shopping days in our town, a day when most people went to the local marketplace, or *pijaca*, to browse and select, then haggle for the best price on their key supplies for the week. Next to the *pijaca* was a beautiful park with sturdy old oaks as tall as the sky, their branches as thick as a man's waist.

Everyone making their way to the *pijaca* had to pass by the park, which also housed a charming day care center. The building was picturesque, looking more like a castle out of a fairy tale than a '70s socialist day care. The women who worked there took great pride in creating an environment that was warm, beautiful, and educationally enriching for the children. With its tall oaks, idyllic day care, kind teachers, and happy kids, the park always had an aura of magic and tranquility—it was like being in an enchanted forest permeated with goodness and peace.

That morning, the children playing outside in the park during recess were shocked to discover the body of my grandparents' neighbor twitching in the shadows of an ancient oak. The screams of the preschoolers were heard by dozens of townspeople walking by on their way to the *pijaca*. The teachers had tried to mobilize the children away from the body, but a couple brave young boys were already scaling the tree.

A crowd was gathering and growing now, watching in disbelief as the boys climbed the massive oak in an effort to free the man. Gasps erupted as the crowd watched the rescue mission unfold before their eyes. Some shouted to let the bastard die, some encouraged the boys to work faster so he could live, and all the while the teachers shrieking and begging the boys to come down. Eventually, the scene ended with a loud thump as the body dropped onto the soft spring grass.

The man was not dead. He had been saved once again by the city's people, this time some of its youngest residents. I can only imagine what he must have felt, walking home through town again, disheveled, scared, and disoriented. According to the local gossip, his body fell like a ripe plum. Having no experience with plums or orchards, I didn't understand what this meant but imagined his body burning for days afterward with a dull but persistent pain and various shades of shame.

After this, the man sequestered himself in his home and was neither seen nor heard from again. He had probably given up on being able to do anything right, including taking his own life. I imagined this, too, was a source of great disappointment to him, only adding to his sense of past failures.

In the end, I was glad the gossip about him ceased. I continued to occasionally check for signs of suicidal tendencies in my grandparents, like giving away prized possessions—in their case a pair of new slippers or some fishing bait—but thankfully, there was no indication of this. My grandparents seemed to hold onto and enjoy the things they loved best, and my vigilance gradually relaxed. As the days grew warmer, my thoughts turned to splashing in the Adriatic Sea.

# FRIDAY
## Mornings

O n Fridays and Sundays, producers from surrounding villages converged on our town, selling everything from fruits and vegetables, to livestock, to cars, bras, housewares, and cheese. The vendors knew their products intimately. If you were buying a pig, the farmer could tell you exactly what the animal had eaten—acorns, perhaps, or the sweet, ripe plums growing abundantly on his property.

Cheeses came to market bearing the unique flavors of the grasses the cows had pastured on. Some bore hints of violet, some of marigold, some, sweet dandelion. Dairy farmers brought warm, unpasteurized milk to town on their bicycles, fresh from their cows and goats, and were always eager to explain its nuanced flavors.

Over the years, long-standing relationships developed between farmers and their regular customers. Egg producers took great pride in bringing still warm eggs directly to the homes of their top buyers, including my grandmother. The eggs would be warm to the touch and flecked with feces and feathers. They were the best eggs I've ever eaten, with the most orange, almost red, yolks I've ever seen.

I loved the intricate knowledge the farmers shared with us and the relationships my grandmother had cultivated over the years to ensure the highest quality food for our family. She was a model homemaker and took immense pride in procuring and preparing our food. Part of this process was the elaborate ritual that unfolded each week in our home. Every Friday morning, my grandparents would venture to the *pijaca* to purchase a piglet. Other items would be bought as well, but the focal point of the Friday shopping was definitely the piglet.

My grandparents always bought the same thing—a young animal, no more than ten kilos, to ensure the proper ratio of fat to muscle. It wouldn't be old enough to have developed large reserves of fat, and its meat would be perfectly textured for roasting.

Buying livestock at the local market was the most common way of procuring the best and freshest meat. On Friday mornings, I'd awaken to the sound of neighbors dragging their pigs home from the market. I grew accustomed to the sound of squealing pigs, and over the years it came to signify the familiarity and comforts of my childhood. My grandparents' arrival back at the apartment would be signaled by more intense squeals and the kicking of the pig on the bathroom floor.

My grandparents would kill the animal in their bathroom, in the tub. They had all the required equipment for at-home slaughter: a razor to shave the hair, a crescent-shaped knife for slitting the throat, various other knives for cutting and carving out specific body parts, and endless containers for the liver, brain, lungs, intestines, and so on. The process itself was brief. Front door to death's door was about fifteen minutes.

The slaughter of the animal didn't upset me. It was a custom in our culture to know your food. Children in the country grew up with chickens, pigs, goats, or cows, understanding full well that the animals would be slaughtered one day, humanely and with as little pain as possible, to provide nourishment for the family.

City children had frequent opportunities to see live animals as well and had a similar understanding that this was food. There was nothing gross, awkward, or unnatural about it. Animals were well cared for while they were alive and were killed with dignity. Their meat was enjoyed and helped sustain the cycle of life. In those days, food wasn't something that came from a grocery store exclusively—it was an involved, dirty, and rewarding part of life itself. Often a beautiful part.

Following the slaughter each Friday, our dead piglet's internal organs would be collected into various containers for immediate preparation that day. Then the animal would be cleaned and salted and readied for a trip to the local shop where it would be roasted on the spit. While my grandfather took the piglet to the shop, my grandmother would set about cleaning up the bathroom.

I imagine liters of bleach and other chemicals being used to fully scrub out any residue of blood or flesh. My grandparents were exceptionally clean people in general, but this was a different level of clean. This process took longer than the actual slaughter. I never watched my grandmother clean the bathroom, but the smell of strong chemicals was overwhelming. This was the only part of the act that bothered me—the caustic smell of chemicals. It would permeate the house for hours.

But all would be forgotten that evening when my grandfather would return home with the crisply roasted piglet. The aroma of the delicious meat would fill the house, and family, friends, and neighbors would gather around the kitchen table, salivating, waiting for dinner to begin. My grandmother would have by this time prepared all the internal organs in various sauces, from tomato to garlic, and would start to roll them out. Good *rakija* and wine would be on the table, and finally all would be ready for us to begin.

Before everyone helped themselves, my grandfather would ceremoniously break off the extra crispy tail and an ear of the piglet and serve them to me. They were delicious, and I always felt special to be given such a treat ahead of everyone else. Finally, everyone would dig in, enjoying the love, labor, and sacrifice that had gone into this one meal. And the cycle would begin anew.

*My grandparents on their engagement day, Yugoslavia, 1951*

# WILD
## Strawberry Jelly

For the first six years of my life, my parents rented an apartment in the house of the most prominent priest in our town. Always clad in the black robes of the Eastern Orthodox Church, he was a large man made even more formidable by a glass eye and a long white beard. Children ran to their hiding places when he came into the neighborhood. Adults bowed down, kissing his hand in deep piety. I, on the other hand, ran eagerly to greet him as he returned home from an important day in the parish. He'd pat my head kindly and tell me I'd go places in life.

This vision of my future pleased me—after all, this man would know. His word was law in our town, his comfort and counsel sought by many. Yugoslavia was still a very socialist country in the '80s where religion was discouraged, if not forbidden, but thirty years of socialism couldn't erase centuries of belief. The priest had retained immense power and authority. While he wasn't an official political figure, he presided over key life events, from birth to death, and had the power to elevate or diminish careers. As such, he was both respected and feared.

This feeling extended beyond the priest. Partly by association, partly on her own merits, the priest's wife was widely regarded as the town's authority on everything falling outside her husband's domain. Gardening, general codes of conduct, child rearing, mores on gift giving, principles of cooking and baking, jelly making and the pickling of vegetables for the winter months, customs for weddings, baptisms, and passings—all fell under her purview. She was also learned and well informed more generally, the only woman to have read every book in the town library.

Being a tenant in the house of such a woman brought keen pressure to perform and to maintain a certain high level of conduct. It also brought an opportunity to learn. No one could have been better suited to this role than my mother. Young, driven, energetic, and thriving on accomplishment, she was the perfect complement to the priest's wife, exhibiting excellence and attention to detail in all she did.

Indeed, the two women hit it off instantly, the older woman embracing my mother as her own daughter, taking her under her wing, coaching her, and taking great satisfaction in seeing her master the finer points of life. My mother, for her part, loved the attention, the vast knowledge and experience being imparted to her, and in turn, executed to perfection what was expected of her, much to the satisfaction of both parties. I imagine the priest's wife saw something of her younger self in my mother, and she rewarded my mother's enthusiasm by opening up more and more, selflessly sharing what had taken her fifty years to learn for herself.

In the end, what started as a landlord-tenant relationship grew into a beautiful friendship, and the two women greatly enjoyed the regular visits that allowed them to spend time together and discuss their common interests at length. Picture a Slavic Martha Stewart visiting her star pupil, and you start to get the idea.

Preparation for these visits was always intense. My mother would clean the house top to bottom, scrubbing and polishing all surfaces to a high sheen. She'd starch the crocheted table covers and place artfully arranged fresh cut flowers in every room. No detail would be overlooked, no effort or energy spared.

In return, the priest's wife would notice everything—every little detail would be acknowledged and discussed at length. She'd ask my mother to elaborate on how she'd gotten such a shine on the furniture—did she use a special, perhaps homemade solution? How did she get her plants to look so healthy? How did her Turkish coffee taste so fine? How did she manage to starch the tablecloth just so, honoring the handiwork that had gone into it while also making it usable and accessible? My mother would practically glow as she expounded on the various topics, growing taller as the priest's wife nodded in approval.

The full sequence of compliments complete, the education portion of the visit would commence. The priest's wife might share a prized cleaning or decorating tip, generally something too intricate for most people to grasp, but my mother would get it right away. Her eyes would light up, and she'd immediately offer an ingenious example of how she'd put it to use.

My mother would be thrilled with what she'd learned, and the older woman would beam to see her protégé absorbing the finer points of her teaching so readily and so well. This full virtuous cycle would unfold in real time before my eyes, each person's energy blossoming into something of value for the other.

Before each of these visits, my mother would sit me down for a serious talk. She'd instruct me, yet again, on how to behave appropriately in her friend's presence. She'd explain how much I should contribute to the conversation and how, when she looked at me certain way, I'd said enough. Above all, whatever I did, I was not, under any circumstances, to embarrass her in front of her mentor and idol. She made it clear she lived for this woman's approval.

*My parents at a birthday party, Kraljevo, 1970s*

One morning when I was about four, we were in the process of preparing for one of these special visits. My mother had gone over the house with a fine-tooth comb, decorating with season-appropriate floral arrangements, starching the furniture covers, and polishing the silver until it gleamed. But this time, as an extra treat, she had also procured a very special wild strawberry jelly from her mother to serve with the Turkish coffee.

My mother and I had our obligatory serious conversation, and I was again instructed, in no uncertain terms, on how to behave around her friend. In essence, less was more. Any sign of my mother widening her eyes at me or giving me the look and I was to cease all conversation and politely excuse myself. It wasn't clear to me where exactly I was supposed to go, or if I was supposed to go anywhere at all, but I was afraid to ask for clarity on this point.

That afternoon, the priest's wife arrived. She greeted me kindly, asking how I was doing, whether my summer was going well, and if I had a lot of friends in the neighborhood. I answered truthfully and to the best of my ability and saw my mother nod in approval. Each satisfied with this brief exchange and my exemplary behavior, the priest's wife and my mother moved into the living room and started chatting.

Their friendship had surely blossomed over the years—they were clearly very fond of each other, practically able to finish each other's sentences. As usual, the priest's wife made note of every effort my mother had put into the visit, and my mother received the praise from her mentor with deep satisfaction.

When an appropriate lull in the conversation came, my mother explained that for this visit she had procured some wild strawberry jelly from her mother and would be serving it in a minute with the coffee. It was common knowledge that wild strawberry jelly was very hard to make, involving both days spent gathering the strawberries in the forest and hours spent washing and cleaning them and cooking the jelly.

Wild strawberries were minute compared to their ordinary cousins, making the preparation time and effort especially intense. The flavor was also more delicate. Only a very experienced homemaker would get the sugar to acidity balance right while maintaining the full integrity of the fruit's flavor.

I sat at the living room table listening to the wild strawberry jelly conversation. The two women were deeply engrossed in it, now ignoring me. They went on endlessly about the difficulty in preparing such a treat, about the effort and the know-how, about this, that, and every imaginable aspect in between. I was beginning to lose patience with the topic and sensed the frustration building within me. Another few minutes passed—no change of topic. Not a single look or word to me. Not even an inquiry as to whether I might like to try this wild strawberry jelly myself. Nothing. I was invisible.

Finally, my mother brought out piping hot Turkish coffee, a crystal glass of chilled water, a small container of wild strawberry jelly, and a single silver spoon—all presented on a silver tray topped with a crisp white doily. She placed it in front of our guest. As my eyes traveled across the tray, my anger escalated. Only one spoon. After I'd been listening to them go on about it for what seemed like an eternity, I was not even going to be allowed to taste this forbidden fruit. Forget about angry, I was incensed.

The priest's wife admired my mother's presentation, commenting in too great detail on how she loved the way everything was arranged—the special touches, the starched doily, and, infuriatingly, the way the wild strawberry jelly was presented with the single silver spoon. This was getting to be too much. My head was spinning. Were they *trying* to piss me off?

The priest's wife picked up the single silver spoon and directed it toward the small wild strawberry jelly container. Without realizing what I was doing, I leapt from my chair, dove the distance of the living room table toward our guest, hacked up every bit of phlegm in my throat, looked her right in the eye, and spat victoriously in the jelly. Surprised, she jumped out of her seat.

My mother shrieked and put her hand over her mouth. I too was stunned. I didn't comprehend the full extent of what I'd done, but I knew it was bad, very bad. The priest's wife recovered first. She reached out to me gently, patted me on the head, and smiled. I didn't know what to make of this. My mother, on the other hand, was beet red and began excusing my behavior in sentences that didn't make a lot of sense.

Our guest commented simply and wisely that these things sometimes happen with children and that it was quite all right. I, however, knew that nothing was all right. The rest of the visit went by in a daze. I don't recall anything else that was said or done. I was deep in worry over my upcoming punishment. I knew this was the worst thing I'd done in my young life so far and that my mother had suffered terrible damage as a result.

Finally, the priest's wife got up to leave and politely bid me goodbye, careful not to mention the incident. My mother walked her out. When she returned, she seemed tired. I was glad to see this, hoping she might not have the energy to inflict a proper punishment. When she finally spoke, she simply pointed out how disappointed she was in my behavior, how poorly it reflected on her and the family, and how it had caused her pain.

I started to cry—not tears of anger, fear, or even relief, as I'd expected, but tears of sorrow, regret at having hurt someone I loved so dearly. For the first time in my life, this feeling, dark and terrifying, washed over me. It was as if a thousand waves were crushing my little heart.

My mother must have seen the despair in my contorting features. She gently put her arms around me, allowing the simplicity of a hug to bond us again and set things right. Choking on my tears, I collapsed into her arms and resolved never to do such a thing again.

# BLOOD-STAINED
## Cigarettes

While I rarely ventured into the upper stairwells of my grandparents' building, I was familiar with every stone, crack, and crevice of the two I traveled each day. I knew which step met the next at a sharp angle and which had a more rounded connection, perhaps due to the heavier hand of the mason who had laid it down. I would imagine the man's hand growing weary as he worked the mortar, making the corner less exact.

The complex had been built by laborers who were part of the great migration to the cities that followed World War II. They'd helped build schools, hospitals, and housing projects throughout Yugoslavia. I imagined young masons working thirteen-hour days laying the stone and railing that would become my grandparents' stairwell. I imagined them thinking of their families in far-off parts of this newly formed, now free country and longing to be reunited with them.

I always wondered what became of these young men. Were they still laying stone, just somewhere else in this beautiful country still marked by so much pain? Or were they retired, perhaps working their fields back home? Did they ever wonder who was traversing the stairs they'd built so many years ago or think about the wishes and aspirations these people might be carrying in their souls as they moved up and down?

The stairwell was always cool and a bit drafty in the summer, smelling of musty basements, cucumbers, and jasmine. In the winter, it smelled of fried onions, heat mixing with vapor from the radiators, and cabbage cooking on the many stoves in the building. I loved coming in, wet with snow and outside chill, and being wrapped in its familiar aromas. It was my gateway to the safe and enveloping world of my grandparents' apartment, and I loved everything about it.

There was one thing, however, that puzzled me—the cigarette butts in the corners of the stairs. There were never a lot of them, but enough to cause me concern. And it wasn't the butts per se, but the blood. What on earth was it doing there?

Not all the cigarettes had it, which was even more baffling. The number was always around half. I also noticed that some blood stains were darker than others. This was curious, too. Did different people have different colored blood? Were some people sick? Maybe children had lighter blood that became darker as they got older. This detail, in particular, troubled me—I wondered endlessly about the color of my own blood and how it might change with age.

These finer points were incidental, though, and the larger question remained—why were about fifty percent of people bleeding from their mouths? It was something straight out of a horror movie. As my mind turned over the possible causes, I considered the very real possibility that black magic was in play. Black magic was an integral part of life in the Balkans. A product, no doubt, of our many conquerors, it was augmented by our pagan roots and fortified with a pinch of Slavic soul, which thrives on obscurity of reason.

Whatever the cause, magic was everywhere, and it could be used as a very plausible explanation for anything—from your aunt remaining a spinster to your uncle's poor harvest, from your neighbor's sick dog to her unfaithful husband. Whatever the circumstance—loss of life, love, or job—magic would always be cited as at least one possible cause, instantly absolving the person involved of any personal responsibility, or liability for that matter.

Given such tendencies, there were a number of everyday magicians, known as *vracars*, who operated in our area. A typical *vracar* would be part shaman, part guru—expert in everything from divination and healing to the casting and removal of spells. It was not deemed irrational or embarrassing to seek their counsel or ask their help, either in removing black magic that had been "put" on you or weaving a spell to effect your desired outcome.

These magicians were busy people. They lived in large, richly appointed homes. Some charged a flat fee, but most simply asked that you donate whatever you felt was appropriate. I had trouble reconciling how a client might choose to "donate" nothing or very little knowing full well that the magician had the power to ruin their life, their marriage, their health—basically cause full-on destruction of everything they'd ever held dear—if they didn't come up with the right amount. I decided that most people were sensible in such matters and that this was what led to the nice homes of the *vracars*.

*With my grandparents at a neighbor's, Kraljevo, 1970s*

In the case of the bloody cigarettes, it seemed unlikely that half our town's population was sick and bleeding from the mouth. I also ruled out the possibility that they were smoking following a visit to the dentist (this just didn't make sense as most people had terrible teeth). This left black magic as a very real possibility. Half the town's population had either been unlucky enough to have had a curse put on them or cheap enough to have offended a magician with too small a donation.

I set out to follow the situation more closely, carefully observing neighbors and others for any sign of possession or illness as they made their way up and down the stairs. I worried that, whatever the curse or ailment might be, it seemed to spread easily and might be contracted by my family or myself.

My efforts were rewarded one day when a woman entering the building took the last drag on her cigarette and flicked it to the floor, crushing it underfoot. As she disappeared up the stairs, I ran eagerly to examine the cast-off butt. As I leaned down to look at it, my mouth spread in a slow smile. The cigarette was indeed covered in blood—the same shade as her lipstick.

# PUDDLE
## Under My Chair

My paternal grandfather was a kind, gentle man known for his wisdom and patience. It was the kind of wisdom that comes from having suffered war wounds, the horrors of a German death camp, and the loss of a child. The kind of patience that allows one to find not only meaning in adversity but the will to march on and live again. Growing up, I didn't understand any of this, but I had a deep respect for my grandfather. I noticed his kindness to everyone, especially us children.

While I loved my grandfather dearly, I could sometimes be a nuisance. I remember him taking me out for a walk in the park one beautiful spring afternoon when I was about four. We strolled under the trees, enveloped in the gentle breezes of spring. The day was perfect. Nature was stirring all around us, ripening and teeming with life. The scent of jasmine, fresh cut grass, and cherry blossoms filled the air, and light poured through the trees in patches, lending a dreamlike quality to everything.

After a couple hours of walking, we spotted a small café situated among thick trees. We sat down in the shade to rest and continue our enjoyment of the day. Not having been to many cafés in my short life, I didn't know what to order, so I went with the waiter's suggestion of apricot juice.

We didn't drink juice at my house, so when I tasted it, it was new and unbelievably delicious, sweet with a little tang of sour and cooling as it went down. I decided to have another, and when the waiter brought it, I downed it quickly, smacking my lips. Why didn't my parents buy me juice at home, I wondered. I decided to speak to them about it. This was too good not to enjoy on a regular basis. On that note, the waiter appeared again, offering me another apricot juice. Why not, I thought.

As the waiter moved to clear the juice bottles from our table, I spotted some men enjoying an afternoon break over beers. Their table was filled with beer bottles, their cheer evident in frequently erupting laughter. Our table only had two bottles with a third on its way. It seemed empty, devoid of merriment. I decided to turn that around and make our table as festive as theirs. I told the waiter to leave the bottles, and when he arrived back, my juice in hand, I promptly ordered another.

The waiter brought my juice and moved on to the men's table. I watched the bottles accumulate as he served them another round of beer. Even though the men outnumbered me and my grandfather was only having coffee, I was determined to keep up. I asked my grandfather to summon the waiter, and I ordered another apricot juice. I downed it as soon as the waiter set it down. It still tasted delicious, but my mind was now too preoccupied with the task at hand to focus on flavor. Before the waiter left, I asked for another apricot juice.

As the afternoon wore on, I kept yelling out to the waiter every few minutes to bring me another juice. He looked to my grandfather for approval, and each time my grandfather nodded wisely. So the waiter brought me one bottle after another.

After this had gone on for some time, I could see I'd leveled the playing field considerably. The number of bottles on my table was much more in line with the number of beer bottles on the men's table. It felt good. I was starting to feel a sense of exhilaration, and I could smell victory.

In the sweet moment of this realization, I also realized I was feeling uncomfortable. My bladder was full. I tightened my muscles and turned my attention back to the men, watching for their next move, planning mine in response. They just sat there—talking, laughing, enjoying their beers. No new rounds at the moment. Good.

Not so good was the increasingly painful feeling of my very full bladder pressing on my internal organs. I was beginning to feel nauseous. My grandfather, seeing something was wrong, asked if he could help—if I perhaps wanted to use the restroom. Absolutely not, I said. I was not giving up now, so close to victory. No way was I leaving the battleground simply to use the toilet.

But the pain was really strong now. I began to squirm in my seat, press my legs together, and shift from side to side in hopes of managing the discomfort. But nothing seemed to help—it was only getting worse. My stomach was beginning to bulge out, heavy with the weight of the apricot juice. Now the waiter, too, kindly offered to escort me to the restroom. I wondered if he was in league with the men

*My paternal grandfather at Christmas, Kraljevo, 1980s*

at the other table and trying to throw me off. I declined his offer and ordered another apricot juice.

This time, as the waiter brought it, I took my eye off the game for a second to glare at him. In that moment of defocusing, I dripped a few drops of urine in my underwear. It felt pleasantly warm and lightened my discomfort for a second. In the next instant, the floodgates opened fully, and I peed in my chair. I peed for a long time, feeling the pleasurable relief as the pressure and pain drained from my body.

The waiter screamed at me. I was still peeing, and it felt good. The urine was beginning to puddle around the waiter's shoes. He yelled at me again, but I was undeterred.

My grandfather gently asked the waiter to lower his voice and bring me some napkins. The waiter and I were both shocked at my grandfather's civility. The waiter returned with the napkins, still stunned at what was happening in his café. He tried to explain this was a family establishment, a place of repute, and that "acts of defecation" were not allowed. I didn't know what "defecation" meant, but something in his tone made me want to order another apricot juice, so I did.

I remained seated in my chair, its cushion heavy with urine, my shirt now wet as well as the moisture made its way upward, absorbed by my remaining dry clothes. Before I could finish my juice and order another, the men paid their bill, got up, and left. I quickly assessed the number of bottles on each table. Yes, I had won!

Then, in one fell swoop, it was all over. The waiter cleared the beer bottles from the men's table and carried them to the kitchen. Upset, I jumped off my chair, my pants sagging.

As if nothing had happened, my grandfather paid the bill, thanked the waiter kindly, and promised we'd be back again. On the way home, we talked about everything but my embarrassing behavior. I was still having a great day with my grandfather.

It all came to an abrupt end, though, when I got home and my mother saw my clothes. While my grandfather had preserved my dignity at the café and on the walk home, there was no escaping my mother's wrath and the reality of what I'd done. The day ended with a stern scolding, a stronger than expected pat on the bottom, and my promise never to do it again. I fell asleep that night lying in my warm, dry bed with a smile on my face, thinking back on my moment of glory at the café—and the wonderful day I'd had with my grandfather.

# GYPSY
## Magic

Yugoslavia had a long, wild, at times bloody, history. As a key trade route linking East and West, it had served as the gateway to Europe for the Ottomans, Muslims, and Communists. It was also a major chess piece in the great game of world dominance, starting World War I and redefining the landscape of the Balkans, Europe, and the world in the process.

The result was an incredible diversity of peoples—*narodi i narodnosti*—all with their own unique customs, their own superstitions and beliefs. And all those people, over so many centuries, had woven their magic into the land. Growing up, one heard the most astonishing stories of fairies, black and white magic, and sorcerers with fantastical powers.

While magic was deeply ingrained in the culture, when it came to magic, no group was more feared and respected than the *Roma*, or gypsies. The fear probably stemmed from lack of meaningful contact with the population at large. The gypsies lived nomadically, appearing under bridges or on the outskirts of town. Their makeshift settlements consisted of a few cars or wagons, lines of brightly colored laundry criss-crossing the air between them. They entered our world to beg or tell fortunes on market days and to entertain on Sundays.

I, like others—especially children—feared gypsies. I was afraid they'd cast a magic spell on me to stunt my growth or melt me into soap. The story went that gypsies kidnapped local children, melted them into soap, and sold them in far-off lands. I wasn't sure which would be worse, being torn from my home, parents, grandparents, and the life I'd known or being melted into soap. Why soap I didn't know either, but I wasn't about to ask—I just needed to concentrate on not being captured.

My most common interaction with the gypsies came on Sunday afternoons when they came to the large quad of buildings where my grandparents lived to entertain, bringing dancers, musicians, and a massive brown bear. The unlikely spectacle of bright colors, exotic dance, and a wild animal in the courtyard of our otherwise normal socialist complex was surreal. I loved it.

Knowing that most "proper" families had their elaborate Sunday lunch at midday, the gypsies always arrived around two or three in the afternoon, just as people were finishing up the meal and looking for some entertainment. Dressed in red, orange, green, and hot pink, anywhere from a handful to over two dozen people would stream into the courtyard.

Their music was a combination of the Eastern European songs I knew and loved and Far Eastern sounds new and exotic to me. The instruments varied, but I remember the blast of the tuba, the quintessential gypsy instrument, generally accompanied by guitar and violin, with some kind of percussion keeping the beat. The overall sound was rhythmic, inviting, and sensual.

The star of the show was a giant brown bear. All the neighborhood kids shrieked with excitement at the sight of it. As the music announced the arrival of the troupe and the bear, children dropped whatever they were doing and rushed to their balconies to watch. Unless it was your birthday week, seeing the bear would be the highlight of your week.

The gypsies always started with acrobatics, jumping through hoops or balancing balls on their heads, all set to the loud thumping of their mystical music. As the acrobats performed, children and women started to dance, their bodies awakening to the music as if entranced.

Our gaze darted from the musicians to the dancers to the acrobats as we grew more and more engrossed in the spectacle, our little eyes widening with each movement, each beat. A few songs in, the main act commenced and the bear took center stage. By this time, all the families in the complex were hanging off their balconies watching the show unfolding in the courtyard.

The bear started off by dancing—shaking, turning in circles, and skipping from side to side. It was incredible to see such a large animal move with such grace. Typically, he'd do a few tricks, imitating a man putting on a hat or a woman applying makeup or using a mirror. Then he'd get on a unicycle and ride around the courtyard.

As he approached each balcony, children squealed with a mixture of pleasure and fear. I remember hardly being able to contain myself on these Sunday afternoons, my little heart pounding madly to the beat of the drums. The bear was ten, fifty, perhaps a hundred times my size and only feet away from me. Thrilling.

The climax of the performance was always the same. The bear picked up a violin and started to play, ratcheting up the excitement. Then the musicians joined in to support the maestro, the dancers clapping their hands and motioning the observers to follow suit. A minute later, the spectators were on their feet, in the moment, clapping rhythmically and participating in the spectacle, tapped into some universal stream of happiness.

At the end of the performance, the bear always bowed to his audience, and the gypsy children took off their scarves and went balcony to balcony collecting tips. People on the lower levels threw coins into the scarves, and those higher up threw their money directly at the bear.

I collected coins all week long so I could personally reward this excellent afternoon show. I was always careful not to throw coins at the bear's face, though, for fear of accidentally hitting his eye and blinding him. The image of a decrepit, one-eyed bear, combined with the distinct dread of gypsy retribution on his behalf, sent a chill through my heart. I didn't even want to think about it.

At the time, I too was just part of the crowd moved by this incredible performance. But as I look back on the experience now, I find it remarkable. Rarely did we invite the gypsies into our world, but these brief moments were an invitation into theirs. Their ability to move us, physically and emotionally, transporting us to a place where we could find a common thread of happiness despite our differences, was truly magical. Perhaps this was the true magic of the gypsies.

# KEEPING
## the House in Order

My grandparents loved their apartment. They loved decorating it, beautifying it, and relentlessly cleaning it. Wallpaper would be redone, floors polished, wood trim cleaned and painted, new curtains hung, towels and sheets ironed and starched—all way too frequently.

While their home was a sanctuary that brought them both great joy, they had different ideas about how best to enjoy it. My grandfather craved alone time at home, liking nothing more than being with my grandmother, just the two of them, in the space they loved so well. My grandmother, on the other hand, loved nothing better than opening her home to friends, inviting her group of "ladies" over for coffee and conversation. Always exceedingly well behaved, they'd sit together for hours in my grandparents' dining room—knitting, gossiping, sharing recipes, and swapping stories of their children and grandchildren.

My grandmother was a skilled homemaker, and for these occasions she'd pull out all the stops. Watching her go to such lengths, I had to think there was a bit of friendly competition among the ladies as each took her turn as hostess for these gatherings. I had observed something of this in the course of their conversations. One might say that her daughter was getting married, and another would share that her daughter had not only recently married, but was already expecting. Or one might say she'd made cherry jam, while another might, in a friendly way, share that she'd made watermelon jelly, which everyone knew was infinitely more complex to prepare.

The gatherings would be scheduled in the evening, around six o'clock, so as not to disrupt the steady, predictable pattern of my grandparents' days. They'd

followed the same routine since their early forties when my grandfather had retired from the military. Each morning, they'd rise, make the bed, dust the bed-
room, and share a cup of Turkish coffee over which the daily shopping list would
be finalized. Then they'd visit the market and arrive back home in time to prepare
a three-course lunch, always served at noon on the dot, probably a habit from my
grandfather's military days.

Lunch would consist of soup, meat, a vegetable, and dessert. Lunch without
meat was unthinkable and would not be considered a meal. There would also always be a batch of fresh hot peppers on the table for my grandfather. They were a
favorite of his, and I recall him eating as many as eight or ten in one sitting just to
amuse me. After lunch, my grandparents would clean up meticulously and retire to
separate rooms. There they'd read their daily newspapers and work collaboratively
on crossword puzzles, with me shuttling inquiries back and forth.

Three to five o'clock was nap time. It was commonly understood that no
phone calls were to be made or received during this time, ensuring peace and
quiet, the only sound the vague humming of my grandfather's radio, tuned to a
station playing the melancholy music of his native Bosnia. This music always made
me introspective and a bit sad. It was the song of remote rural plains, fearless winds
whipping them, and the uncertain fate of the Bosnian people.

Finally, after five, the household would awaken. It was now time for dinner, socializing, and strolls along the *korzo*, the main artery of town where young and old

*With my grandparents at a wedding, Kraljevo, 1984*

*My grandparents at a wedding, Kraljevo, 1986*

would come out each evening to get some fresh air and reconnect with friends.

My grandmother's evenings with her lady friends were always a big production, and the days leading up to them felt festive. My grandmother would plan the extensive menu of baked goods, organize the ingredients and baking supplies, and finally prepare each individual cake, cookie, or torte lovingly and with great care.

She and my grandfather would go through the house with a fine-tooth comb, dusting the tiniest of miniature figurines, polishing all the wood furniture, and combing the fringes of their Turkish *cilims* so they all faced the same way. My grandfather would take special care with the dining room table and chairs, polishing them over and over to bring out the deep reddish color of the wood. The final touch would be placement of massive bouquets of fresh flowers, purchased at the *pijaca* and painstakingly arranged by my grandmother.

The evening of the party, baked goods would be carefully laid out on beautiful platters, with silver serving utensils all pointing in the same direction to enable the guests to help themselves with ease. My grandmother would get out one of her many coffee sets, taking care never to use the same one twice in a row. Each set would have its own story, this one a wedding gift, that one the prized possession of a maiden aunt.

My favorite stories were those that involved faraway places—Egypt, Damascus, Istanbul. I'd fantasize about visiting their busy bazaars, rich with the aroma of spices and exotic flowers. I'd picture the shoppers themselves, haggling and smiling broadly as deals were struck and packages exchanged hands. I longed to participate in these *souks*, and my mind worked overtime conjuring up images.

Once the house and cuisine were set, my grandmother would take great care getting herself ready. I loved watching her pick out her attire for the evening—she'd always select a new dress or housecoat to reflect the season—and seeing the genuine excitement and anticipation in her eyes.

One evening, one such party was upon us. Everything was perfect, and even the weather had cooperated. It was a mild May evening, and the scent of linden trees in bloom mingled with the smell of vanilla and spice from the baking.

My grandmother looked beautiful in a button-down dress patterned with tiny bouquets of flowers in purple, white, and yellow, her favorite color. The dress flattered her figure, showing off her striking legs, and she could have passed for a woman fifteen years younger. I had the feeling her appearance reflected her state of mind that evening, content with her life and overjoyed to be sharing it with good friends.

As the ladies arrived, they immediately remarked on the beautiful apartment, fresh flowers, and new décor. They complimented my grandmother on her appearance and, as the food and coffee were served, raved about her baking and hosting skills, praising her generously and sincerely.

I could see a spark of deep appreciation in my grandmother's eyes and feel the warmth in her heart for such dear friends. Always a self-proclaimed people person, she genuinely loved others and wanted to do good by them, whoever they were. So this was special. An evening when it all came together, perfectly, just as she'd hoped and planned.

The ladies carried on an animated conversation for a couple of hours, sharing the latest in their children's lives, showing photos of their grandchildren, and eventually touching on the economy, the price of flour and onions, the ever-galloping inflation, and their plans for the summer.

The evening would probably have continued along these lines for at least another hour were it not for my grandfather. I could see him tossing and turning in the armchair in the next room, puffing under his breath, flipping the pages of the daily paper more and more abruptly. It was unclear what was bothering him, but I realized it had something to do with our visitors. As the laughter of the ladies increased or the conversation became more impassioned, his breathing became louder and I was sure I could hear him cursing under his breath.

Then all of a sudden he stood up and dumped the paper on the table, storming into the dining room where the gathering was taking place. Predictably, as soon as the ladies saw him, they greeted him festively and started peppering him with questions. How was he feeling? Had the fishing season started? Had he exceeded any of his hiking records of late? And how was *Partizan*, his favorite soccer team, doing this year? They complimented him on his ever-fit physique and remarked on his tan, which contrasted strikingly with his blue eyes. Just sweet, friendly ladies trying to be polite and find some common ground.

My grandfather at first answered their questions with a brisk "yes" or "no" followed by silence and glares back at our guests. Initially, the ladies didn't think much of it. But as the questions grew less frequent and the silences longer, it was apparent something was wrong. Finally, the ladies stopped asking questions altogether and just stared at him. He stared back, scowling now.

My grandmother, watching the situation grow stranger by the minute, tried to shift attention back to herself, muttering, "Don't mind him, he must be tired." She started off on another topic, and within minutes the ladies jumped back in, holding up their end of the conversation, my grandfather's awkward behavior forgotten.

Laughter and lightheartedness returned to the room—only to be shattered a few minutes later by a piercing whirling noise. Everyone started. The sound was at once familiar and out of place. Within seconds the ladies were jarred by sharp whacks to their legs and feet. Their stockings ripped under the onslaught. They shrieked and jumped out of their seats: my grandfather was vacuuming around them.

It took a second for everyone to process what was happening. My grandmother, visibly upset, yelled at my grandfather to stop. He ignored her and continued vacuuming, focusing even more intently on getting every last bit of dust out of every fiber of the carpet. The atmosphere was growing unbearable, not to mention loud.

Finally, satisfied with the disturbance he'd caused and seeing the ladies starting to collect their things, my grandfather ceased further cleaning. In an effort not to end the evening on such a strange, unpleasant note, my grandmother put on her best smile and offered another round of coffee and *slivovitz* to settle everyone's nerves. Hesitantly, the ladies accepted, probably feeling too rattled to actually walk home anyway. The conversation picked up again, and the ladies moved on to the next topic.

This peace, too, was short lived, interrupted this time by the astringent odor of cleaning solution and the surprised shuffling of guests around the dining room table as my grandfather started scrubbing vigorously under and around elbows and hands as they rested innocently on the table. The ladies were again shocked, lifting their wet hands and forearms abruptly, trying to wipe the noxious chemical from their skin and clothing. My grandfather was undeterred and continued cleaning.

Eventually, the confusion turned into a full-on stampede out of the house, the ladies grabbing their purses and rushing out the door. My grandmother remained

*My grandparents in their dining room, Kraljevo, 1993*

seated at the dining room table, her head in her hands, her hurt and disappointment palpable. My grandfather didn't seem to notice. He collected his cleaning supplies and left the room. I had no idea what would happen next.

Eventually, my grandmother regained her composure and started picking up the plates and coffee cups and clearing the dining room. To my surprise, my grandfather showed up immediately and started cleaning right alongside her. He helped her stack every plate, lift every crumb from the table, and collect every knife, fork, and spoon.

His patience was astounding. In sharp contrast to the abrupt man from half an hour ago, he was now unbelievably calm, working peacefully and productively beside my grandmother. The two of them struck a rhythm of back and forth between the dining room and the kitchen, working tacitly, efficiently, in concert like two bees. I couldn't believe it.

Finally, the house was put back together, restored to its pre-guest tranquility. The evening was advanced by this point, but before going to bed, I saw my grandfather approach my grandmother and give her a gentle hug. He tenderly, if briefly, told her how glad he was that she was back with him, and that the house, their nest, was back to its normal order. No ill feeling remained, and the two partners, lovers, bees, went off to bed, in harmony once again.

# THE ANGEL
## of Syphilis

My grandparents' home was a loving environment that soothed and sheltered me. Once inside, I was enveloped not just in their love, but in the local gossip, as well. I grew up listening to running updates on our neighbors' lives, from speculation on extramarital affairs and the latest romantic matches, to a recounting of recent deals scored at the *pijaca*.

The gossip was generally harmless and invariably entertaining. Occasionally, though, less pleasant topics arose, from disease and death to black magic. Straddling all three categories for me as a child were the relentless stories of the sexual exploits of our neighbor's daughters—the same neighbor who had tried to hang himself first from a willow by the river, then from an oak in the park.

Still very much a child, I didn't know the young women in question or grasp exactly what it was they were doing. But the neighbors were upset. They spoke of open sexual promiscuity, unfolding largely in the foyer and stairwells of our apartment complex.

Some complained of running into the young women engaged in sexual acts in the entrance to the building. This was especially uncomfortable as the space was by no means large and my grandparents' neighbors often had their grandchildren with them. This led to uncomfortable conversations about what they'd observed, how it all worked, and so forth. Very awkward.

Others were embarrassed that the women solicited men, generally farm workers from depressed towns, at local train or bus stations, bringing them back to the apartment building to render services. The worst part was that, as they were soliciting these unfamiliar men, the women would publicly acknowledge and greet their neighbors, thus establishing a connection between themselves and the fine, upstanding citizens of the complex. Outrageous.

The other part the neighbors didn't like was the alleged syringes discarded in the stairwells. They said the syringes were from penicillin shots the women were giving themselves to cure syphilis. Though I'd never seen any with my own eyes, I was terrified by this aspect of their degenerate behavior and made a point of carefully navigating the stairs for fear of stepping on these used, diseased syringes.

It was unclear to me why the women would be administering medical procedures themselves anyway and at night no less. Didn't they, like the rest of us, have access to free medical care at the local clinic? Or was their condition such that the shots had to be given at the time of their nightly trysts? Although I didn't really understand what syphilis or penicillin were, or trysts for that matter, the syringes begged the question of broader public safety, including mine.

In light of all the scandalous gossip, I envisioned the women as wraithlike and ravaged by disease. I pictured them with loose, yellowing teeth and tufts of hair missing, their bald spots covered with open sores oozing whatever nasty pus syphilis produced. I imagined their bodies emaciated, their skin gray, probably wrinkled and hanging despite their youth, their eyes red with fever, their smiles demented. All in all, as no one thought to inform me that one couldn't get syphilis from touching the same railing or doorknob as a diseased person, I lived in more or less constant fear of the women, their syringes, and their disease.

This all changed a few years later when I overheard someone in town speak kindly of the women. Apparently they were known outside the complex for their beauty and goodness. Needless to say, this came as a bit of a shock. While I had trouble reconciling my neighbors' and grandparents' accounts with this much more positive one, my faith in humanity eventually won out, and I created a very different picture of our neighbor's daughters in my own mind.

I imagined rushing up the stairs to my grandparents' flat one day and bumping into a beautiful young woman. Both of us are startled, but she regains her composure quickly, coming down on one knee to look me in the eye. She is stunning, with glowing hair the color of wheat, clear green eyes like fresh water running over mossy stones, and a broad smile showing strong, white teeth. Beyond her alluring physical presence, she projects a sweet, soothing nature and an aura of calm. She is the very image of a fairy from the tales my parents read to me when I was small—the only thing missing is the magic wand.

She speaks to me kindly, solicitously, taking my small hands in hers and asking if I'm all right. I am more than all right. I am beside myself, having had this wonderful encounter with this most beautiful and magical of creatures. I leave in a daze, knowing something special has happened. My life has been touched by an angel.

As I enter my grandparents' flat, I am visibly changed, causing them to wonder. When I tell them about my impromptu meeting, they recoil in horror—I have met one of the two sexually deranged women! My grandparents become more and more agitated (after all, I've been exposed to one of the most deviant people they know), but I remain calm. As they ponder the possibility that the woman has somehow influenced me, perhaps infecting me with abnormal sexual desire for strange men and probably syphilis as well, I feel a sense of relief. I am released from the grip of fear and can now navigate the world outside their apartment with freedom and ease.

As I look back on the gossip surrounding our neighbors' daughters, I'm sure some of it was true. Some sexual encounters probably did take place in the building—how often I'm not sure, but probably any frequency would have been too much for its residents, mostly pensioners. The men they solicited probably were mostly transients—had they been townspeople, someone certainly would have recognized them, and no one ever mentioned any names. And the women probably did meet them at the bus or train station as they were arriving or passing through town.

As for the rest, I have my doubts. To this day, though, these women capture my imagination. Sometimes I seem to remember hearing they were teachers, and that they, to the best of everyone's knowledge, took no money for sex. I reflect on this bizarre combination—educators by day and altruistic sex workers by night.

Other times, I remember my ideal version of the story, the one where the women represent light, beauty, all good things—the things we aspire to, or are elated or moved by. I imagine that this is what the men found so alluring. The sense of comfort, refuge, magic. With no access to the real story of my neighbors' lives, they become the angels of my own, guardians rather than destroyers of the safe, loving world of my childhood.

# THE SUICIDE
Cult

While I never thought suicide was common in our town, I was struck by two cases taking place within months of each other when I was twelve. The first victim was the mother of a family friend. From what I overheard, she was about my grandparents' age, a seemingly stable and happy woman. Judging from the gossip, there was nothing striking about her life or the months leading up to her death. In fact, a lot of people felt it was a big gossip letdown that she'd killed herself without some big cause—no cheating husband, no domestic abuse, no alcoholism or illness.

But the woman did have a cause, and she said so herself, in her suicide note. She had been living with her daughter and had predicted correctly that her daughter would be the one to find her. When the young woman walked into the house that day, she saw her mother hanging from the ceiling in the hallway, a step stool by her feet. On the ground was a note that read, "I did it because of you."

A few short months later, our town was rocked by another suicide or, more accurately, a double suicide. Two fifteen-year-old high school students were found dead, the time of their death synchronized. They were best friends from good homes, good students and all-around good girls.

Some said it was just a case of good kids, having too much going for them, going wrong. Others thought the girls had been spoiled, that they'd had too little parental supervision and too much time on their hands. I personally didn't know the young women, but I made sure my grandparents were spending as much time as possible with me—no way was I going to risk it.

In the days that followed, rumor had it the young women had joined what was known as a *sekta*, or cult. No one was exactly sure what cult, what its teachings might be, or which cult members had been indoctrinating these particular girls. The latter was the biggest mystery of all. In our town, everyone knew everyone else. There were no strangers. So who had brought the teachings of the cult to our town? Who might be harboring its secret members? People became vigilant, paranoid.

Initially, I didn't think too much about it, but as more and more people talked about this mysterious cult, I grew curious. Who were these people leading innocent girls to their deaths? Where did they come from? If I saw them, would I know them for who they were?

As the stories swirled, my grandparents grew more and more concerned. Finally, they sat me down and told me we were going to have a serious talk. First, they told me they loved me and that I was the apple of their eye. I had known and felt this my entire life and found it daunting that they were bringing it up now—clearly, this was going to be serious.

My grandparents then asked if anyone strange had approached me lately. I thought carefully about this, then considered it even more deeply, feeling this was appropriate given the severity of this very serious conversation. Finally and honestly, I answered no. They seemed relieved.

Then they asked if anyone had, in a tricky way, asked me to join a cult. Again, I thought very carefully. I realized that no one had really asked me to join anything—not a cult, not a team, not a popular clique, nothing. I told them so.

They were skeptical. They told me these people are subtle and may have asked in a way that eluded me. I thought about it some more, but the answer was clear—no invitations had come my way. I was beginning to feel a bit left out. Was something wrong with me? Why was I not special enough to be invited to join the cult? I didn't even care what kind of cult it was or what they preached. I just wanted to be asked. Disillusioned by this apparent lack of interest, I was beginning to feel resentful.

My grandparents continued our talk, asking if anyone had offered me any drugs. Again, no. No one had offered me anything. Not drugs, not ice cream, not even gum. Nothing. These cult people were really starting to piss me off. Who did they think they were—something special? Not to even offer me anything. I was upset now. I was more than upset, I was enraged. I made up my mind to find these people, wherever they might be hiding in our town, and reject them. After all, this was my turf—they had no standing here. I would seek them out and reject them to their faces.

My grandparents, satisfied with my answers thus far, offered some tips on how to act if approached by cult members. One, they said, don't respond and don't look them in the eye. Two, don't accept their invitation. Three, don't take anything from them, especially not drugs. Definitely not drugs. Four, don't follow them to their cult nest, for if I did, I'd be trapped and wouldn't escape with my life.

However, if I were to fail at instruction points one through four and find myself trapped, I was to do whatever it took to escape. I was to think more broadly than just using the front door. This puzzled me as most of us lived in high-rise buildings. It followed that the seat of the cult would be similarly situated. If I were to escape without using the front door, that would only leave windows and balconies. Were my grandparents suggesting I jump to my death?

*My grandparents at an event, Kraljevo, 1974*

When I tried to gain further clarity on this point, they glanced over my question and continued with point five and onward. But I wasn't really listening anymore. I was trying to decide which would be better—jumping to my death from the window of a high-rise or, under the influence of the cult, killing myself like the two girls.

As our serious conversation came to an end, my grandparents seemed pleased with the result—I seemed reflective, meaning I was taking in their words of wisdom and processing their advice. But nothing could have been further from the truth. Instead, I was furious with the cult for having absolutely no interest in me and was contemplating the escape options should I ever be entrapped.

The days rolled on, and a few months without any suicides passed. No one had approached me, and no invitations to join the cult were forthcoming—nothing. It was all very frustrating at first, but eventually I decided there was no use waiting around. I accepted the fact that I just wasn't cult material (whatever that meant) and went back to my simple life as a happy, if too unsophisticated for a cult, child.

# STRANGER
## in the Bed

A branch of my mom's family came from a small city in central Serbia where their ancestors were among the town's original settlers. The family had lived in the heart of the city ever since, watching the town grow up around them for many decades.

Maybe it was the city itself, where people weren't as guarded as in our town, or perhaps it was their nature, but either way these were big, huge-hearted people. They were the kindest souls I'd ever met, always having a soft spot for someone in need and ready to lend a helping hand when you needed it. They'd be the first to laugh with you when you were happy, to strike up a song when you were celebrating, or to cry with you when you were sad.

My cousins accepted life as it came, with open arms and hearts and very little in the way of provisions or planning. There was always drama in their house and there were always strangers, sharing my cousins' woes, hardships, and space. This could be anyone from a newly transplanted teacher, to a farmer bringing his goods to market, to a random traveler passing through town.

The teacher would hail from some far-flung part of the country. She'd have just gotten a new job in the big city, needing a place to stay for a few days until she settled in. She'd be the third cousin of a colleague's wife from a decade ago who'd landed this job and somehow thought of my cousins and reached out to them for help. She'd be a bit naïve, kindhearted with big hopes and dreams. Perhaps she'd be too young to have married, or not very attractive, or with some slight disfigurement, but they'd say, "She has a good heart—we'll find her a husband, too!"

The farmer would be in town to sell vegetables, or cheese, or livestock, needing a place to rest before the market opened or before catching the bus back to his village the next day. The random traveler would be a young man from some other far-flung part of the country, on his way to find work or get a bride. They'd have stumbled upon him at the bakery that morning and taken pity on him, offering him a night of rest before he continued on his way.

The teacher would be eager to hear the local gossip—to find out who had the best price on eggs and who was an alcoholic or wife beater. The farmer would be looking for an "in" with the townspeople so he could sell more onions, cheese, or cattle. He'd also be looking to secure a regular stall at the market, and my cousins would know who could help. The weary traveler would be in search of a home cooked meal, someone to listen to his tale, and a warm bed to sleep in. My cousins were always willing to provide refuge and a shoulder to cry on. Their home was the proverbial safe house of humanity.

The other thing I remember about my cousins' house is that it was always enveloped in smoke—thick, gray cigarette smoke. It was everywhere, and I often wondered how they saw each other through it. They were all smokers, and their impromptu guests, it seemed, also all smoked. Life's injustices, the world's problems, personal wrongs—all were hashed out and resolved at their kitchen table, shrouded in smoke.

Not surprisingly, there had been a few incidences of fire, mostly due to visitors falling asleep while smoking and setting themselves and the bed alight. Thankfully, no one had been seriously hurt over the years. They'd just gotten into the habit of budgeting for new beds on a more regular basis.

Even though my cousins' house was often pure chaos, I always loved visiting. Each stay was an adventure—full of strange dialects, passionate conversations, engrossing stories, and every flavor of deep emotion. This was in sharp contrast to the orderly, organized life my grandparents led. Our world was proper, calibrated, predictable. Visiting the cousins was anything but. It was like going to the circus—you never knew what you'd see next.

I remember one visit in particular. We called the cousins a few weeks in advance to see if the timing was convenient and confirm our dates. They'd be thrilled to see us, they said, and we were looking forward to seeing them, too.

Preparations for the trip commenced immediately. My grandmother bought gifts for everyone—coffee and cigarettes for her brother-in-law, dress material for her sister, makeup for their girls, and chocolate and sweets for the younger children. She spent a great deal of time carefully picking out each present, wrapping it, and packing it safely so it would look presentable upon our arrival.

Next, she bought us each new pajamas, then washed, starched, and ironed them.

She got herself a new housecoat and me a new dress, one that showed off the gains I'd made in height and beauty. Then we bought our bus tickets and called our cousins to let them know exactly when we'd be arriving, with which bus company, and how many suitcases to expect.

*Me at a Belgrade park, 1978*

Finally, the day of the trip was upon us. We woke up bright and early to get a head start. We both took a nice long shower, did our hair, and got dressed in our finest. My grandmother put on her makeup, and we made the bed, made sure the house was in order for our return in a few days, and set off early to the bus station to allow plenty of time to get there and wait for the bus. My grandparents felt it was best to arrive early rather than rush, so we gave ourselves a comfortable hour cushion before our bus was to depart.

Surprisingly, the bus was only 45 minutes late, and the trip itself was uneventful. We found good seats and were happy to find the driver sober and in a decent mood. He only made one stop for lunch and a few beers. This gave my grandmother and me a chance to get some water and a snack. We decided against using the public toilet due to an infestation of flies and the lack of toilet paper and doors on the stalls.

Happily back on the bus, we chatted about the upcoming visit and our eagerness to see our cousins. It was going to be great. Despite the initial delay and break for lunch, we made very good time. Thanks to the driver's exceptionally fast driving and general disobedience of the rules of the road, we were only fifteen minutes late.

Upon our arrival, strangely, there was no one at the bus station to greet us. This was especially odd since we'd confirmed our travel dates with our cousins weeks in advance and had been assured someone would be there to meet us. We were even fifteen minutes late, which would have given them even more time.

My grandmother was clearly vexed at this lack of responsibility and planning, mumbling under her breath about how disorganized the cousins were, how it had been a mistake to believe they would ever be on time. Finally, some thirty minutes later, a cousin showed up, in an excellent mood and more than delighted to see us.

His chipper demeanor served to neutralize my grandmother's displeasure, and we all set off happily for home.

At the house, we were greeted by the perpetually billowing smoke, walls more discolored than in previous years, and cousins more aged. The yellowish-brown stain of tobacco was evident on them, as well as on the house. While everything was a shade darker—their skin grayer, teeth more yellow and missing—their spirit was as upbeat and welcoming as ever.

They were delighted to see us, thrilled that we'd pay them a visit. They inquired about my school, our health, my parents, our town, my grandfather's fishing, his hiking, our neighbors, everything. They couldn't get enough of our updates and would frequently come around the kitchen table to plant big kisses on my cheeks.

These overt expressions of love were odd to me but, along with the genuine interest the cousins showed, made me feel special. They hung on our every word, laughed heartily at every story, and enveloped me in hugs and attention. I loved it—these people were great! I felt a bit guilty that my grandmother had been so displeased with them earlier and hoped all was forgotten.

The day wore on, and as afternoon approached, my grandmother and I were growing a bit tired from the trip and the day's events. We were hoping to take a nap. Our hosts were more than happy to oblige. I was drowsy from the bus ride and all the attention and was looking forward to collapsing into nice, crisp sheets. We thanked our hosts and, under their direction, headed for the guest room to get some much-needed rest.

But as we made our way into the room, someone jumped out of the bed. The three of us looked at each other in shock. My grandmother and I had never seen this man before. Dressed in traditional farm garb, the stranger seemed groggy. Clearly he'd never seen us before either and was assessing our intentions. Who were we and what were we doing interrupting his sleep?

My grandmother regained her composure first and screamed at the top of her lungs that there was an intruder in the house. A moment later, one of my cousins appeared. We all looked to her for an explanation. With a broad smile and hearty laugh, she apologized and introduced the man as family from another town.

My grandmother and I continued to look at her. As it turned out, she really didn't know the man's name. He was from a village of their ancestors—a good, honest man in town to sell chickens. Somehow this didn't reassure us. What? What was he doing here? In our bed? In our room? Now? For my grandmother, especially, this level of carelessness, if not outright rudeness, was not to be borne.

My cousin told us calmly not to worry, the man at times came over to rest and would be getting up now to head to the market. And indeed, now more at ease, the man thanked our cousin and bid us all goodbye, sloppily making the bed behind him. He said he'd be back on Friday.

My grandmother recovered her ability to speak and, after insisting the sheets be changed before her very eyes, calmed herself down. Eventually, the day did end, but not before my grandmother had our return date changed to Thursday.

# HOTDOGS
## and Hemophilia

Like most kids when I was growing up, I loved *virsle*, the Serbian version of hotdogs. We never had them at home, but I'd eat them at friends' houses or for lunch at school. Their absence from our home menu never struck me, in the same way I'd never noticed we didn't consume much pumpkin or chicken, or very many sweet potatoes for that matter.

But the absence was abruptly brought to my attention one day when, without thinking, I mentioned how much I'd enjoyed the hotdog I had in school that day. My mom's brow furrowed. Her face grew grim. "How often do you eat hotdogs?" she asked accusingly.

This took me by surprise. Why would she be interested in this one specific food item? I could tell something was wrong but answered truthfully: I had hotdogs once or twice a week, depending on what the school kitchen served and whether my friends' parents offered them.

Then, in a show of defiance, I added that I liked them. My mother positively shrieked at the news. It wasn't clear whether she was upset about the consumption of hotdogs in general or just my enjoyment of them. I quickly scanned my memory banks for any specific information instructing me against either. Blank. Nothing came to mind.

Her hands on her hips, my mother gave me an angry, but also worried, look. Then she pulled me close to her and pushed my hair back from my forehead, looking for something. Lice, I presumed. After a few minutes of intense scrutiny of my hairline, and evidently not finding what she was looking for, my mother asked if I was feeling all right. Other than feeling confused and like I'd done something horribly wrong, I was feeling great. I had been feeling especially great before this awkward conversation.

Finally, my mom knelt down and looked me in the eye. "Never eat hotdogs again," she said. This was followed by a long silence. Then she told me she loved me. Excellent, I thought. I still wasn't sure how hotdogs, love, my hair, and the general level of consternation, disapproval, and worry currently in the room were all related.

Then she dropped the bomb: "Hotdogs cause hemophilia." Wait, what? For starters, what was hemophilia? A type of lice? Whatever it was, it was not good, and she said if I kept up my current "lifestyle," I could get it, too.

My internal alarm bells were going off. I tried to quickly compute how many hotdogs I'd eaten so far in my life. Twenty, thirty, fifty, a hundred? I was getting dizzy with arithmetic and becoming increasingly panicked that whatever the number was, it was way too many. I started sweating. I had the feeling something terrible had happened—to me, by my own hand, but without my knowing.

My mind started to race, trying to assess the extent of the damage. I wondered if I'd committed similar health offenses by eating other foods—peas, perhaps? Seeing my confusion, my mom explained that hemophilia was a very serious blood disease and that hotdogs, made with subpar meat and chemicals, could lead to it. This was getting worse by the minute. Now I might have a serious blood disease.

I had so many questions. How many hotdogs did one have to eat to get this hemophilia? Was it curable? Did other foods lead to it? Because I'd like to stop eating those immediately, as well. Furthermore, why hadn't anyone said anything earlier? Why did my friends' parents feed us this terrible food? Were they trying to kill me? Their own children? Was the school trying to poison us? Tomorrow I must share this information with my friends and check their hairlines for any strangeness.

I spent the rest of the day in a daze. The next morning, I shared the bad news with my friends. They laughed at me and told me my mom was wrong. Given the shock of the prior day's news, I was too worn out and weak to defend my mom's assertion and gave up on championing my no hotdog campaign at school.

Still, for the next month, twice a day, morning and evening, I carefully examined my hairline in the mirror, looking for anything unusual. I also carefully monitored my heath for any unfamiliar changes. Most of use, I swore off hotdogs for life.

Fast forward thirty years. I'm on vacation with my new boyfriend in Puerto Rico and suddenly I'm confronted with the hotdog quandary. Innocently, clearly without knowledge of the hotdog to hemophilia correlation, my boyfriend brings us hotdogs for lunch. I freeze. The child in me asks, "Is he trying to kill us?" The adult in me tries to calm the child down and reminds me it's thirty years later, I'm in a different country, and I've never really come across any supporting evidence for the whole hotdog-hemophilia connection.

Seconds, then minutes, pass. My boyfriend kindly offers me the hotdog again, probably assuming I just didn't hear him. I'm about to say I'm not hungry, or make some other superficial excuse, but I pull myself together. I decide to let my adult self manage the situation. I put on a charming smile and, at the risk of sounding very strange, I tell him the full story.

He listens carefully and, when I'm done, bursts out laughing. Just as it was back in second grade, the story is comical. But this time the laughter encourages me. Instead of remaining focused on the obvious dangers of the hotdog-eating lifestyle, my mind opens to a new possibility. Perhaps there really is nothing to the tale my mom told me. Perhaps it isn't true and I can resume eating hotdogs. My boyfriend assures me that this is indeed the case.

By that afternoon, my lunch still untouched and my stomach twisting with hunger, the transformation is complete. My unwavering fear of hotdogs, based on a single conversation with my mother at age eight, is now dead.

To celebrate, my boyfriend gets me a fresh hotdog in a steaming bun. I hesitate for a moment, but the late hour of the day, my hunger, and the will to get beyond what now seems like a wholly irrational fear win out. I devour the hotdog. It tastes divine. The processed meat and bun melt together in my mouth, hints of mustard and ketchup registering in the background. I order another one, then another, and then one more.

I am stuffed. And happy. And relieved. My body is satiated, my mind free of its decades-long fear. For the rest of that vacation, I eat hotdogs for lunch every day. I feel like Forrest Gump breaking out of his braces and starting to run.

# THE ENGAGEMENT

My mom's sister was a vibrant, exceedingly attractive nurse well known in our town for her panache and enthusiasm for socializing. A much sought-after guest at town gatherings and celebrations, she'd always be the first to strike up a conversation or to lead her enchanted tablemates to song.

Given her social nature, my aunt had been blessed with many suitors. But after a decade or more of dating, she was now in her early thirties and still single. Though no spinster by any means, she was starting to feel the pressure to marry and start a family. This same pressure weighed on my grandparents—especially my grandmother, who wanted her daughter to find the man of her dreams so she could experience true happiness and the joys of motherhood.

The only problem was that, after so many years of dating, there wasn't anyone left in our town for my aunt to date. The men were either already taken or too young or too old for her. Thankfully, just as she was facing this predicament, an eligible, thirty-something professor moved into town. He immediately began to circulate socially, getting to know all the suitable women in the vicinity. The situation was perfect for my aunt, who instantly made it to the top of the list.

The two of them met, promptly struck up a mutual liking, and started spending time together exclusively. Each valued the other's unique contribution to the budding relationship. My aunt brought social connections, charisma, fun, and a sophisticated sense of style. The professor offered intellectual and professional accomplishments, financial security, and standing in the community. Both parties were mature enough to appreciate the complementary, symbiotic nature of the union.

The professor hailed from Sjenica, a smaller, less prosperous city in the south of Serbia. Its people were known to be honest and hardworking. They took pride in the long and turbulent history of their town. In the Middle Ages, Sjenica had served as a resting place for traveling merchants and an Ottoman stronghold. More recently, it had played a pivotal role in the Serbian Revolution and seen intense fighting during World War II.

The professor's mother and brothers still lived in Sjenica. The professor took great pride in his roots and the fact that, following his father's death, his mother had raised and put all three boys through college singlehandedly. The professor himself had been the youngest PhD in his field, had taught overseas, and had a distinguished martial arts career under his belt. All in all, he had a lot to be proud of, not least of which his Sjenican roots.

As weeks and months passed, the romance between the professor and my aunt was progressing nicely. They were clearly very enamored with each other, and the rest of us enjoyed seeing them so happy. Both had enough life and dating experience to know whether the relationship had a future, and it was clear that it did. In the interest of time and practicality, they were headed for the altar.

And so it was set that the professor would come over one evening to ask for my aunt's hand in marriage. We were all delighted—my aunt beside herself with happiness and anticipation, my grandmother thrilled that her daughter would soon be engaged.

Leading up to the big night, my grandmother and aunt worked overtime to clean the house and prepare a feast. No expense or effort was spared. Windows and curtains were washed and the furniture was polished to a sheen. You could see your own reflection in the dining room table.

My grandmother put together a fine menu for the occasion. The best twenty-year-old *rakija* was to be served, followed by a rich assortment of *meze*, including prosciutto, various homemade cold cuts, young and aged cheeses, and the finest baked goods. Next would come the main course of a piglet roasted on the spit, accompanied by roasted red peppers in garlic vinegar, stuffed cabbage, rice, green beans, two home-baked breads, and an excellent red wine. For dessert, there would be a nutmeg and pecan torte, an assortment of miniature sweets, coffee, and aged apricot brandy.

The evening the professor was to arrive, my grandmother sat me down, as the only child in the family, and explained that this was to be a big, happy, momentous occasion for my aunt and that it was our collective job to do our best to support her in getting engaged. So no interrupting, no asking for anything, no detracting from the event in any way. This was my aunt's night, and it was my job to reflect well on her.

*With my parents at a wedding, Belgrade, 1980s*

My grandmother sat my grandfather down for a similar conversation. In his case, however, the coaching was to behave in an appropriately engaged, warm, and welcoming manner. He was not to ignore our guest, watch TV, or read the paper. Above all, he was not to delve into politics, and under no circumstances was he to talk about the refugees storming our town from the south.

The refugee problem was definitely being felt in Kraljevo as droves of people were coming north, competing for the town's limited resources and jobs. Most of the townspeople didn't like this and often complained, sometimes bitterly. But given my grandfather's lack of interest in politics and the local economy, it seemed safe to assume he wouldn't follow suit.

The professor arrived at the appointed time, visibly happy and eager to claim his bride to be. My aunt looked as beautiful as ever, and the rest of us were dressed in our best. Though the preparations had been intense, with everyone feeling like they needed to be on their best behavior, in the end everything fell into place and everyone seemed to get along effortlessly and beautifully.

We all enjoyed meeting the professor, and he seemed pleased with our company as well. There was no lack of laughter or conversation, and, like any good guest, he repeatedly complimented my grandmother on her cooking, her home, and the overall pleasant experience.

As the evening drew to a close, I could tell he was getting up his courage to finally ask my grandfather for his daughter's hand in marriage. Up to this point, my grandfather had been quiet, generally ignoring the conversation and watching TV in the background. This had gone unnoticed as the rest of us had been busy chatting away.

Finally, the professor addressed my grandfather directly and respectfully asked for his approval and blessing to wed my aunt. The rest of us fell silent, delighted to have come to this point in the evening and keenly awaiting the response.

The air was thick with anticipation. I saw a tear roll down my grandmother's face as she sat witnessing this joyous event. It was after all a perfect match, we all liked the professor immensely, and my aunt would have a good life with him.

Much to our surprise the silence persisted. A minute passed and then another. Nothing. I blinked my eyes and angled my head just to be sure my ears weren't blocked and I hadn't missed anything. I hadn't. Nothing had been said, and nothing was being said. Just silence. Utter silence that was now weighing on the room. It was beginning to feel heavy and suffocating.

More minutes passed. My aunt began to shift in her chair and cough lightly in hopes of inspiring her father out of his trance and on to a quick "yes" so that her life could continue to unfold happily. It didn't come. By now, my grandmother had turned in her chair and was staring at my grandfather. He sat there calmly, undeterred, focused on the soccer program on TV. She was beginning to turn red.

The professor was plainly confused. Later, he told us he had been wondering whether or not he'd actually uttered the question or had said it loud enough. The explanation for this kind of rudeness could only be something simple, something benign like my grandfather not hearing.

More minutes passed. The professor repeated the question. This time, my grandmother placed her hand on my grandfather's shoulder, kindly but firmly drawing his attention to the table and the question before him. My aunt was on the verge of tears.

Finally breaking the silence, my grandfather faced the professor, looked him straight in the eye, and said, clearly and loudly: "I can't believe these damn people from Sjenica coming to our town and stealing our jobs and women." Then he fell silent and turned his attention back to the TV.

Everyone gasped. My aunt shrieked in horror, her future life, love, children, and home all vanishing before her eyes. This was unrecoverable. The professor blinked a time or two, in shock as well. To the best of everyone's knowledge, such an outrageous insult to a guest, much less a suitor and potential son-in-law, had never been uttered in our town. How to proceed? Or to proceed at all?

We all waited for the professor's next move. I could see the internal debate playing on his face. Should he get up and leave, storm out offended and insulted? Should he defend his people and show his pride? Should he argue politics with this man? Or should he simply repeat the question?

Being an intelligent, even-handed sort of person, the professor repeated the question. Not missing a beat, my grandmother delivered the desired "yes" herself and popped a bottle of champagne to celebrate.

The roughest patch of the evening successfully bridged, the engagement was consummated and the day ended with hugs and kisses all around and my grandmother sweetly calling the professor "son-in-law." My grandfather took it all in stride and never said another word about it. In years to come he pretended the whole thing had never happened.

# WHOSE
## Shit Is It, Anyway?

The place where snow-capped mountains meet the azure waters of the Adriatic, Montenegro is one of the most dramatic and beautiful of European vacation destinations. Nestled between Croatia, Bosnia, Serbia, and Albania, it dates back to the sixth century and boasts 183 miles of coastline, 45 miles of which are beaches. Looking out at its snow-covered peaks while swimming in the gleaming waters of the Adriatic is one of my favorite childhood memories.

My parents bought land in Montenegro in 1980 and started building a vacation home. The process took over a decade and was executed in spurts, mostly during our summer vacations so we could help with and supervise the work. It was generally expected that our summers would include at least one major improvement to the house. One year it was the red-tiled roof, another, the parquet floor, the next, painting the interior walls. And one year in particular, it was installing a larger septic tank to accommodate the growing circle of family and friends who visited each year.

Each summer, like clockwork, as the weather grew warmer so did the frequency of calls from friends and family we hadn't seen in years, or at least months. Initially, they'd call simply to say "hi"—to check in on us after the long winter, inquiring about our heath, my education, or my parents' work. Then, as the warmth and length of the spring days increased, so too did the intensity of calls. Now they'd want to know when we'd be at our summer home and for how long as they'd love to stop by for a quick visit.

Inevitably, this would turn into a two-week minimum stay with a new excuse each day for why the visit needed to be extended. These would range from a surprise transportation strike back home, to running out of money for a return

*With my father and cousins, on the Adriatic, 1970s*

ticket, to not feeling up to making the long trip back just yet. If nothing else and as a last resort, they'd announce their previously perfectly healthy children were benefiting from the favorable Mediterranean climate—it was soothing their asthma. Everyone's children seemed to have asthma that required at least a two-week cure on the banks of the Adriatic.

Needless to say, our home was always packed beyond capacity, our days busy with various relatives and friends sharing in our summer experience. This constant overcapacity had consequences for the new house, chief among them the need for a larger septic tank. With so many people around each summer, there was no ideal time for such work, so my parents decided to simply ask our various visitors to comply with a few small requests.

As the summer advanced, work on the new septic tank was proceeding according to plan with minimal impact on the home's residents. But finally we reached a critical point when, in order to cure the walls of the tank and solidify the structure, absolutely no solids could enter it.

My parents explained this to everyone and spelled out clear expectations for the following day: for a couple of hours in the morning, the single bathroom was not to be used, and, in the event of an emergency—there were children in the house after all—it was to be used only for peeing. Absolutely no other activity could take place, period. This was critical. If we were to continue to enjoy the house and the summer without suffering an outbreak of hepatitis, everyone would have to comply with this restriction.

I personally saw no issue with it. It was just a couple of hours. I imagined everyone felt the same and could discipline themselves, making appropriate provisions to bridge this small amount of time. To ensure that absolutely no solids got into the tank, the workers building it asked that we physically disconnect the bathroom from the tank by removing a portion of the pipe connecting the two. While my parents weren't wild about the idea, the workers insisted, explaining that, in their experience, someone always disobeyed this one rule, negating all the work they'd put in and costing them numerous additional hours to fix it.

My parents pleaded with the workers, explaining that everyone in our household was responsible, that even the kids would be coached and monitored by their parents to guarantee no solids were flushed down the toilet. My parents said they could vouch for each person's integrity. The workers were not buying it, though, and dug in their heels on this point. Finally, having no choice, my parents relented, giving in to their request.

The night before, my parents reiterated expectations for the following morning and specified the hours. We all gasped and shook our heads at the idea that anyone would violate this one simple rule. Everyone agreed that it was absolutely unnecessary to remove the piece of the pipe. We were all mature individuals or children with responsible parents who could manage this on their behalf. A number of our guests were very nearly insulted by the suggestion of anything otherwise.

My parents tried to smooth things over, saying it was just a couple of hours, we were yielding to years of experience on the topic, and better safe than sorry. Finally, my mom proposed that, to keep everyone out of the house and the bathroom—and everyone's mind off the topic—she'd serve an elaborate breakfast on the terrace that morning. This should occupy us for the specified period of time and allow the work to be completed properly.

The following morning, as agreed, the workers removed a piece of the pipe connecting the bathroom to the septic tank. Everyone watched. My parents were displeased that the missing piece was so close to the terrace where we were planning to enjoy our breakfast that morning. The workers insisted it was the simplest part of the plumbing to remove and that we just had to put up with it for a short time. The decision made and the pipe removed, we all set about helping to prepare and serve breakfast, fully mindful of the restriction on using the bathroom.

It's a strange feeling knowing you can't do something. The more you think about it, the more you feel like doing it. It's like being told you can't use the lavatory during takeoff or landing on an airplane, or no food or coffee the morning

*On the Adriatic, Budva, 1986*

before a blood test, or no carbs on an Atkins diet. It's all you think about, all you crave, all you want or need to do.

The fact that there was a piece of pipe missing in front of us was a constant reminder. Looking at the ten-inch gap where the pipe should have been intensified everyone's desire to do the forbidden. The missing piece was bewitching, pulling us into its vortex, causing us to hallucinate strong stomach spasms that might lead to bowel movements. It became almost impossible to resist the urge. I fought it by keeping busy, helping my mother finish up preparations for breakfast.

Finally, everything was ready and we all sat down to eat, to enjoy the meal and get our minds off the wretched, all-consuming thought of what we mustn't do. My parents tried to refocus everyone's attention on the beautiful setting: the view of the Adriatic, the bright blue sky, the orange, lemon, and olive groves growing wild around us, the scent of iodine and heat mixing in the air—all promising another gorgeous Mediterranean day.

But the bodily urges proved stronger. People's attention was scattered, their concentration poor. They were frequently bending their necks to look at the missing pipe or glance nervously toward the bathroom. A number of people went into the house to fetch this or that, but everyone returned to the table quickly, eliminating any suspicion of bathroom activity. I could tell they were all pacing themselves to the finish line, trying hard not to think about it.

Midway through breakfast, fatigue set in. Our guests slowed their eating, conversation came to a crawl, and the clinking of silverware ceased. People sat with their arms in their laps, counting the minutes to the moment when the restriction would be lifted. A hush fell over the breakfast table, punctuated only by the rhythmic breathing of ourselves and our guests.

A few minutes elapsed. People seemed to drift deeper into their meditative states, diverting their minds and bodies from any slight pressure on the bowels or bladder, focusing instead on the upper chakras, the higher, nobler realms of consciousness. I reckoned we only had about half an hour before the bathroom could be used again without restriction.

Then the sound of a thump broke the silence—the sound of something not large but solid hitting wet ground. We all jerked out of hibernation, blinking our eyes, trying to process what had just happened. The sound had come from the missing pipe area. We looked over and saw a piece of shit lying on the ground. It had come from the bathroom.

Our initial shock turned to unease. People's eyes darted uncomfortably from one person to the next, lingering questioningly on each face, sometimes a tad too long, searching for the culprit. Older children broke the silent interrogation by exclaiming, "*I didn't do it*" or "It wasn't *me*." The younger ones looked around in puzzlement, not fully understanding what had happened. The women looked disgusted and offended, the men confused.

Mothers started questioning their children angrily, demanding to know who did it. The noise around the table was now high pitched. Whose shit was it, anyway? Who had broken the rule? Offended the good hosts?

*With my father and mother on the Adriatic, Budva, 1970s*

Who was the weak link? Who had embarrassed themselves and their family? Who had done this despicable, distasteful, wrong thing?

Then as quickly as it had come, the tension broke. One person started to smile, then another, and then we all burst out laughing. The guests started to joke and tease one another. Even the workers were satisfied at having been proven right. In the end, the septic tank walls were cured, the shit removed, and the missing pipe replaced. Our lives resumed without a hitch, one batch of guests packing their bags that afternoon and another arriving in the evening—in search of free lodging and the much vaunted health benefits of the Mediterranean.

# Postscript

These stories were born with my son. Uncertain upon entering a wholly new phase of life, I sought wisdom and enlightenment—and a break from the daily routine of feedings, lack of sleep, and disorientation. I was in search of something that would lift my spirit, make me laugh, and transport me, if only for a moment, to another, less tangible, place and time.

While the world in which these stories unfold no longer exists, I still cling to the many lessons it taught me. Because of my fantastical childhood, I know in my heart that life is much more than a sum of mundane survival activities. I know that it's fluid, magical, brimming with love and connection.

This book was indeed the respite I needed. It freed my mind to roam the wild landscape of a bygone era and lifted me on the wings of Balkan stardust. I hope it will do the same for you. Until we meet again, dear reader, I invite you to let the spirit of the fantastical into your own life. May these stories amuse and transport you, sustaining you on your journey as they have me on mine.

*Kraljevo, 1977*

# Appendix: Serbian Proverbs

The Serbian language is rich in proverbs. Many feature images of death and suffering, perhaps reflecting the violent history of the region. Others simply mirror the internal logic of the people, of the land and its many conquerors. Here are a few favorites:

**His feet are as big as baby's graves.** Compares foot size to infant graves. Morbid? You said it. Presumably referencing a time when infant death was commonplace.

**He's crying as if he's being skinned alive.** Suggests an exaggerated response. Clearly, this is not a place for sissies.

**He's carrying his soul in his nose.** Indicates a person a breath away from dying. In this vivid image of death, the soul has moved into the nose, ready to exit the body with the last breath.

**A dead man pays no debts.** Cautions against expecting anything (payment or otherwise) from a dead man, or by extension, someone who isn't present or has chosen not to participate. Probably akin to trying to get blood out of a turnip.

**One devil does not scratch out another devil's eyes.** Suggests that similar people support each other and don't turn on one another. Sometimes said of politicians.

**Don't rush—you're not carrying fire.** You're not about to be engulfed in flames, so what's your hurry?

**Don't eat as if you were eating for whores' souls.** Cautions against eating too fast. Presumably, whores have less soul and therefore require less time to eat.

**A greedy father has thieves for children.** Cautions against vice and suggests a "reap what you sow" cycle. Paybacks are hell.

**That's where God said good night.** Refers to a person, place, characteristic, or situation that's beyond intelligence, inspiration, or help. Could be said of a person who is lazy or a house that's very dirty or disorganized.

**A wife is frightened of her first husband, a husband of his second wife.** Elegantly conveys the dangers of marriage for both sexes.

**A clean pig makes lean bacon.** Cautions against being too extreme. If you trim all the fat from a pig, you'll end up with flavorless, or lean, bacon.

**A foolish fox is caught by one leg, but a wise one by all four.** Notes the correlation between ability and the size of the outcome. In other words, a smart man steals the most, à la Bernie Madoff.

**Warm bed, cold food.** Cautions against comfort at the expense of achievement (which leads, presumably, to the good things in life). If you sleep too much, your bed will be warm, but your food will be cold.

# About the Author

Marija Bulatovic was born in the 1970s Yugoslavia and along with her parents, immigrated to the U.S., just ahead of the 1990s Yugoslav wars and the breakup of the country. She is an accomplished business professional with 15 years of experience driving enterprise business with Fortune 500 companies. She currently lives in Seattle with her husband and son.

*Fantastical: Tales of Bears, Beer and Hemophilia* by Marija Bulatovic is an extraordinary tale of life lived in full, vivid, vibrant color set in the 1980s Yugoslavia captures the spirit of the Slavic soul—passion and melancholy with a twinkle in the eye. It's a mesmerizing memoir that takes readers on a wild and unforgettable tour of a country that has vanished from the map, but lives on in this lively collection.

With a pitch perfect voice, and a keen eye for capturing the absurd, the outrageous, the hilarious, the touching, and the sublime, Bulatovic weaves a rich tapestry. Bears, gypsies, quirky family members, foiled plans, unusual and unorthodox neighbors, *Fantastical* has it all. Lovingly told with an unmistakable fondness and deep affection, *Fantastical* is resplendent with humor, magic, and whimsy.

*Fantastical* charms with its wit, keen insights, and larger-than-life stories. Part memoir, part love letter to a place and a people that lives on in memory, *Fantastical* is irresistible.

An exquisite assortment of stories—each more delicious than the last—*Fantastical* is a tale to be savored.